DIANE ACKERMAN

I Praise My Destroyer

Poet, essayist, and naturalist, Diane Ackerman was born in Waukegan, Illinois. She received an M.A., M.F.A., and Ph.D. from Cornell University. Her poetry has been published in many leading literary journals, and in the books *The Planets: A Cosmic Pastoral*, *Wife of Light*, *Lady Faustus*, *Reverse Thunder: A Dramatic Poem*, *Jaguar of Sweet Laughter: New And Selected Poems*, and *I Praise My Destroyer*.

Her works of nonfiction include *Deep Play*, *A Slender Thread*, *The Rarest of the Rare*, *A Natural History of Love*, *The Moon by Whale Light and Other Adventures Among Bats, Crocodilians, Penguins, and Whales*, *A Natural History of the Senses*, and *On Extended Wings*, a memoir of flying. Her bestselling *A Natural History of the Senses* was the basis for a PBS television series, *Mystery of the Senses*, in which she was featured as host and narrator. She is also writing a series of books for children, the first two of which are *Monk Seal Hideaway* and *Bats: Shadows in the Night*, and she is co-editor, with Jeanne Mackin, of an anthology, *The Book of Love*.

Ms. Ackerman has received the Academy of American Poets' Lavan Award, and grants from the National Endowment for the Arts and the Rockefeller Foundation, among other recognitions. Honored as a Literary Lion by the New York Public Library, she has taught at several universities, including Columbia, Cornell, William & Mary, and Ohio University. Her essays about nature and human nature have appeared in *National Geographic*, *The New Yorker*, *The New York Times*, *Parade*, and other journals.

I Praise My
Destroyer

I Praise My Destroyer

POEMS

DIANE ACKERMAN

VINTAGE BOOKS

A DIVISION OF RANDOM HOUSE, INC.   NEW YORK

FIRST VINTAGE BOOKS EDITION, AUGUST 2000

Some of the poems in this work were originally published in *The Bookpress,
Conjunctions, George, The Michigan Quarterly Review, Poetry, Poetry International,
The Seneca Review, Sites,* and *Travel-Holiday.*

A different version of "When the Deep Purple Falls" was originally
published in *A Slender Thread* (New York: Random House, Inc., 1997).

The Library of Congress cataloged the Random House edition as follows:
Ackerman, Diane.
I praise my destroyer : poems / by Diane Ackerman. — 1st ed.
p. cm.
I. Title.
PS3551.C48I2 1998
811'.54—dc21 97-34464

Vintage ISBN: 0-679-77134-4

www.vintagebooks.com

Printed in the United States of America
10 9 8 7 6 5 4 3 2 1

Contents

NATURAL WONDERS

TENDER MERCIES

CITY OF DREAMS

CANTOS VAQUEROS

I Praise My
Destroyer

SCHOOL PRAYER

In the name of the daybreak
and the eyelids of morning
and the wayfaring moon
and the night when it departs,

I swear I will not dishonor
my soul with hatred,
but offer myself humbly
as a guardian of nature,
as a healer of misery,
as a messenger of wonder,
as an architect of peace.

In the name of the sun and its mirrors
and the day that embraces it
and the cloud veils drawn over it
and the uttermost night
and the male and the female
and the plants bursting with seed
and the crowning seasons
of the firefly and the apple,

I will honor all life
—wherever and in whatever form
it may dwell—on Earth my home,
and in the mansions of the stars.

I PRAISE MY DESTROYER

How can it all end,
the moon making foil of the blueblack sea,
at twilight the sandbars holding lavender
among turquoise shadows,
pastels of water lidded by pastels of sky
and, at angle, moon shimmer snaking to the horizon?
By the dockside, a diver kneels at his tank
to test the regulator, as if taking communion.

How can it all end,
the soccer field in September
where an amphitheater crowd chants
Cosmos! Cosmos! as if to all Creation
and, at the goal mouth, the lyric sway
of the keeper repeats like a mantra
over the lips of the net?

How can it all end,
spring white in the dogwoods,
sunset's purple rigging
bellied high over the horizon,
mating lizards in the yard, and sailboats on the lake
—both with bubble throats?
My lover lies beneath me before a whumping fire:
our own private inferno leaps
in the hearth where logs are piled
like hunks of mutton.
A tight bouquet of sparks
hovers in darkness, as I recall

the day's sensual splendors.
He brushes my draping hair from his eyes.
"You're so alive," he whispers.

How can it all end,
the cabbage whites aflutter
like tissue-paper prayers
lofting to Heaven in a Japanese temple,
the yellow roses numbingly fragrant
and even the spiky conifer
whispering scent?

I praise my destroyer.
The sea turtle's revenge
is to dwell at equal measures
from the grave. Our cavernous brains
won't save us in the end,
though, heaven knows, they enhance the drama.
Despite passion's rule, deep play
and wonder, worry hangs
like a curtain of trembling beads
across every doorway.

But there was never a dull torment,
and it was grace to live
among the fruits of summer, to love by design,
and walk the startling Earth
for what seemed
an endless resurrection of days.

I praise life's bright catastrophes,
and all the ceremonies of grief.
I praise our real estate—a shadow and a grave.
I praise my destroyer,
and will continue praising
until hours run like mercury
through my fingers, hope flares a final time
in the last throes of innocence,
and all the coins of sense are spent.

WE DIE

for Carl Sagan

I

We die despite appointments and feuds,
while our toddler,
who recently learned to say No,
opens and shuts drawers
a hundred times a day
and our teen braces
for the rapids of romance.

We die despite the contracts
and business trips we planned,
when our desk is untidy,
despite a long list of things to do
which we keep simmering
like a pot of rich broth.

We die despite work we cherish,
marrying whom we love,
piling up a star-spangled fortune,
basking on the Riviera of fame,
and *achieving*, that human participle
with no known object.

II

Life is not fair, the old saw goes.
We know, we know, but the saw glides slow,
one faint rasp, and then at length another.
When you died, I felt its jagged teeth rip.
Small heartwounds opened and bled,
closing as new ones opened ahead.
Horror welled, not from the how but the when.

You died at the top of your career,
happy, blessed by love, still young.
Playing by evolution's rules, you won:
prospered, bred, rose in your tribe,
did what the parent gods and society prized.

Yet it didn't save you, love or dough.
Even when it happens slow, it happens fast,
and then there's no tomorrow.
Time topples, the castle of cards collapses,
thoughts melt, the subscription lapses.
What a waste of life we spend in asking,
in wish and worry and want and sorrow.

A tall man, you lie low, now and forever
complete, your brilliant star eclipsed.
I remember our meeting, many gabfests ago,
at a crossroads of moment and mind.
In later years, touched by nostalgia,
I teased: "I knew you when
you were just a badly combed scientist."
With a grin, you added: "I knew you when
you were just a fledgling poet."

Lost friend, you taught me lessons
I longed to learn, and this final one I've learned
against my will: the one spoken in silence,
warning us to love hard and deep,
clutch dear ones tighter, ransom each day,
the horror lesson I saw out of the corner of my eye
but refused to believe until now: we die.

ELEGY

for John Condry

The world is breaking someone else's heart
today, the roses are busily mumbling scent,
all the greens of summer have blown apart

in a mad fandango of blossom, sap, and art—
who could be sad in a season of pheasants?
The world is breaking someone else's heart.

Deer invading the garden like Bonapartes
bring a speckled infantry that's heaven-sent.
All the greens of summer have blown apart

winter's stockade; only your maverick spark
is missing, dear friend, prof, redneck and gent.
The world is breaking someone else's heart.

A hundred hearts at your house today chart
a fitful course through the shoals of grief and lament.
All the greens of summer have blown apart

like your ashes on the lake. My own sorrow starts
small as China, then bulges to an Orient.
The world is breaking someone else's heart.
All the greens of summer have blown apart.

PYRRHIC

"Let go,"
said the onion thrip
blistering
a scallion leaf with eggs.
And the coddling moth
agreed,
"Let go."

So I let go
the elderberry cobs
hairthin
without their antlike fruit;

let go
the maple seeds whir-
wheeling
in the logy dusk;

even let go
the myopic orb-weaver
surveying
its web tremor by tremor.

But the wall-rue fern
said, "Not enough.
Let go."

So I let go
the whole big blooming
confusion,
every colorclad chigger, jot,
and iota,
and pared down
to grubstake, bedrock bottom
where the wasp
of mortality
couldn't raise a bump,

but loss rankled
like chains in the heart,
and the callipygous peach
still said,
"Let go."

WHEN THE DEEP PURPLE FALLS

for Sheila Stone

In the lavender hours after daybreak,
before the sun leapt onto the blue stage of the sky
to begin its light opera of soul-searing heat,
we set out on our bikes to circumnavigate Otsego Lake,
which, encircled by dense forest, lay flat as pounded metal,
thickly gray-purple with a light mist rising,
yet wavering clear like an ancient mirror,

and pedaled hard up a long steep incline,
as the temperature of our bodies and the day rose together,
through deep, soft, atmospheric purples
flickering in the filmy veils of morning,
sparking from iridescent birds and butterflies,
glinting from lichens and mosses,

while within the aubergine drapery of the forest,
twigs crackled, a confetti of light fell through the leaves,
small quick beings darted among the tree trunks,
and an occasional loud crunch or scuffling
led our eyes back a million years, through tunnels
of instinct, to violet shadows we interrogated
for bear or mountain lion or highwayman or warrior,

as a mixed chorus of insects and birds sang out,
oblivious to our cycles, but mystified perhaps
by our talk, laughter, and off-key songs,
or by the sight of a woman with blonde hair
riding a teal mountain bike, and wearing
black shorts with purple chevrons
the color of a mallard duck's underfeathers,

and behind her the same thing but different—
a woman with long black hair riding a plum bike,
her helmet, hard as the carapace of a beetle,
shining with royal purple, a hue Pliny the Elder described
as "the color of congealed blood, blackish at first,
but gleaming when held up to the light," a hue
monopolized by the ancient Mediterranean city of Tyre,
which painstakingly extracted it from sea snails,

a hue so precious that ancient Romans risked death
if they illegally produced it, an imperial hue
rare enough for emperors, potentates, generals
and demigods, and then all at once the demimonde,
when a nineteenth-century chemist mixed
coal tar and alcohol to produce a cheap, colorfast,
eye-trembling dye that the French named mauve,
after the purplish mallow flower, and romanced
as the *couleur de rigueur* of the Belle Epoque—

both of us following a road dusted with loose gravel
spread in winters past, gliding smoothly
beside undulating mountains, which roll the way
a dancer rolls her hips as she sprawls, while shadows
staggered like eighth notes through the woods,
the lake grew calm as cold wax, the sun yellowed
and swelled, as sweat began to seep from our faces,

so we drank long gulps of clear warm water
—from bottles, not the lake water, deepening
to black orchid whenever a castle-sized cloud
drifted over, not the mirage water
shivering on baked macadam up ahead,
not the salt water plumping up our cells
that gives us shape and flow and spirits the mind
through soul journeys, but water captured
from a spring in Vermont we had never seen,
filtered by rocks, as we are filtered
by the sights we see, especially the majestic indigo
of the lake, which the Indians named
"Glimmer glass"—praising the lavender air,
and the night purple convalescing in the forest,

as we pedaled higher along the ridge,
whose outcroppings surged with steamy shadows
of darkest purple, a color elusive in nature,
which I love because of its emotional ambiguity,
and also for the sensuous paradox at its heart,
a mongrel color having no wavelength of its own,
but arising from a blend of red and blue—hot and cold
colors, very short and very long waves of light—

which is why, I suppose, its lush caravan of tones,
running from wisteria bloom to carnal Chinese violet,
so captivates the senses, making our eyes linger
and shimmy, unable to focus clearly, suspended
in a state of tense, softly thrilling, voluptuous calm,
where opposites clash and are subdued,
warring passions resolve into beauty,
and it is possible to reach a point of resolution,

in a color not flagrantly sexual like red,
but ethereal and passionate, igniting all the senses,
a moody color introspective as amethyst,
the color of easily bruised emotions,
the color of a summer garden filled with columbine,
monkshood, foxglove, iris and hydrangea,
the color of wet-petaled, sense-bludgeoning orchids
floating above the teeming floor of a rain forest,

and so allowing all battles to meet and become one
tenderness, we rejoiced as we pedaled into open country
where rich growing fields surrender to the sky
their perfectly ordered rows of corn, with leaves
like ironed green collars and tassels shaking glitter
in the uproaring sun—sights we sometimes savored
with little comment and a few delicate sips of mind;
and yet at other times we wolfed down whole vistas—

yet we both knew the tonic value of the journey
that fell somewhere between pleasure and hardship,
though we are not the sort of people who picnic on pain,
or calibrate fun, but we reveled in working ourselves
through the landscape, which we discovered tree by tree,
with mile after mile of chicory and Queen Anne's lace
bunching in the culverts, pedaling hard though
we were steeped in pure exhaustion, pure exhilaration,
knowing that far behind us in the village of Cooperstown,
shops would soon be unrolling their awnings,
museum doors yawning wide, and the great ladle
of enterprise slowly stirring, as the sun rose high
and the town thrummed with a million colorful intrigues,

but we were panting and pushing and pedaling,
steadily pulling the day up behind us, then changing gears
as sunballs of neon-blinding raced over the lake,
more violet than wet, and we biked toward noon,
not thinking of orange roughy served on the veranda
at a grand hotel, where we would later stare
in amazement at the lake we'd circled, stretching bright
as a spill of mercury under the steadfast sun,
not thinking of showers, or rest, or of any tense,
but happily lost in a long serenade of mauve water,
and the what-will-be somewhere around the bend.

Timed Talk

TIMED TALK

Timed talk is what we seek.
It's brought me to you twice a week
    the past five summers,
spring-loaded Aprils,
    and long free falls.

But we do not measure
by season; in the death hush of winter
    where each rime has a reason
my face becomes a sundial
    counting the hours.

Timed talk is flood and drought.
It's something we both
    cannot live without,
so we meet in the abasement
    of your house:

that independent state
in the deep interior
    where my heart is a favored nation
and there is no embargo
    on tears.

Timed talk is a dowser's art.
When the moon is caught
    in the dark scissors of earth and sky,
you bend the twig of a few words
    and water trickles from my eyes.

Timed talk can be flammable and bleak.
Then the kindling minutes beg for fire.
   I am a powder keg in a lightning storm.
You are a loaded gun
     with the safety on.

   Timed talk is pure mystique.
All I know of you: grown kids, agile spirit,
   past storied with grief,
     grand laugh
   like a wolf saluting the moon,

a passion for novels, Beethoven,
   snapping photographs,
World War II history, exotic voyages.
   From such scraps
     I build your robust image,

knowing nothing of the woman
   whose heart you rent,
if your conscience scolds, or regret bites,
   the frets, the dreams you dream awake,
the sirens that rouse you in the night.

Timed talk. I see you in your finest hours.
   You see *me* in my worst—
troubled, sad, and meek,
   my sun eclipsed, my panorama leveled,
the tigers of my curiosity cowering.

Timed talk is the heart's oblique.
   Skimming along on separate time-lines,
we intersect twice a week
   in a painstaking hide-and-seek,
making do with half-light, half-speak.

Still, timed talk is how we meet,
   across the garden fence,
so to speak, where the borders
      are fixed and the risks are weak,
provided timed talk is what we seek.

REMODELING

Plan a small renovation—a reliable light
in the pantry; deeper shelves
where canned goods tumble;
outlets grounded and brought up to code;
a little packing and shoring
of inner walls, to baffle rodents
that ream out insulation
and claw the best earthwork
into a haberdashery of leavings.

Be prepared to expose everything
down to the guts and bowels.
The sink must go, also floorboards,
plumbing, old heating vents,
miswired switches, closets,
addled smoke detectors,
even hand-me-down crockery
and ponderous fixtures.

Engage a laborer trailing yards of drop cloth,
and dragging tools so heavy
he must work sitting down.
Do not be surprised if he begins
to grow a beard (it comes from
close proximity to sawdust),
or if he removes limbs and organs
to angle deep into tight spots.

On the job, he is transmutable.
It's only after hours, without his spirit level,
that he may become unbalanced
and ricochet off walls
in a private chaos he's bolted tight.

Do not expect the expected
or the unexpected. Anything may surface.
Do not be shocked,
if, ripping out a wall,
the workman finds a pyramid
of used razor blades.
They may have served as ballast,
and even added a little ragtime
to the house's creaks and groans.

Try to remember that, by definition,
an estimate is always wrong
(two months equals two years in dog days),
and that cost quickens with time.
Expense is a river whose rapids never rest.

When the house looks like a stage
for a World War I epic, with pits
and seepages even wolves would reject,
you may forget why you began
this immolation. Use metaphors
of magic, transmutation, and uplift,
order from chaos, gold from fire.

Pretend you are restoring the innocence
of birch, the purity of tile,
the calm of paint, the passion of mortar,
the omnipotence of light.

If you find the workman dozing
beneath a counter, in shadow,
where the leaden sink once hung,
his eyelids trembling with dreams,
his tool belt a jumble
of wrenches and spanners,
do not awaken him
with a tumultuous scream.

Do not rummage through his kit,
though you'll be tempted
by the findings and masks,
lubricants and balms, elixirs,
solders, restoratives, and caulks.
Avoid inhaling the adhesives.
Even a small spill can be volatile,
and you may find yourself
intoxicated by the poignant fumes.

Be prepared for the salvage to wind up
unfinished. A process of any length,
it will be more like turmoil timed,
or an agreed-upon upheaval,
than an elegant, organized, obvious finale.

In joy and relief, do not call the workman
a saint because he plastered well.
Do not imagine he'll tidy up
(for months you'll find stray tacks
and ribbons of quicksilver),
or be surprised by an awkward exit.
Painting himself into a corner,
he may leap through the window,
run into his mirage, and disappear
where blueprints vanish in starlight.

BOUNDARIES

Dawn diver of the infinite, plunging
through brave twilights of anesthesia,
your mind a tumbling mosaic, as you lie
motionless beneath a surgeon's cunning,
prey to a generous amnesia,
afloat between worlds, floating free of words,
all need and sense and eloquence reduced
to a flickering storm on the monitors,

a dozen cities sprawl between us now,
but I can see gloved hands strolling
through the pastures of your flesh,
and hear your heart, that old Caruso,
belting out its song—the lyrics say:

"We live a moment among the new roses,
sighting paradise in a backward glance,"

and tell a tale of soul-journeys and strife,
of pleasure principles and neuroses,
a tale of joy and mayhem I know by heart.
Waiting for news in the suburbs of hope,
I hymn your liveliness as I love my life.

THE SORROW RANGERS

The sorrow rangers take the night by storm,
through gloom they gallop, leather-eyed, through hell,
with hoofbeats pounding in a violent swarm
they race calamity on panic heels
and gouge the earth, leaving a cuneiform
deep and jolting as the grief they feel.
Night folds around them like a bird of prey.

The sorrow rangers camp below a moon
cold and distant as a love betrayed.
Their saddlebags are full of smoke and spoons.
All that's left to eat is the self they flay.
So, singing a mournful firelight tune,
they slowly tap their chests and curse the stars,
with hearts all percussion, all past hurrahs.

WILDFLOWERS

Yesterday, you called me a wildflower,
and I knew what you meant: a free spirit
blooming outside domestic gardens,
precious for that, bursting with color
but destined to be always and irrevocably other.

Perhaps you were imagining the field
by your house where wildflowers struggle
up upon their roots, despite harsh winds
and human traffic; or how, in the wild,
flowers use their softness to crack through rock,
thirsting deep to hidden springs.

Because the wild flowers inside you,
your eyes sometimes melt,
and I feel awe washing over me
as you savor the iridescent wildflower
perched on a leather outcropping
only a few feet away, in a Byzantine land
where winds brawl, tempests toss,
and, driven wild, flowers fly in all directions.

After hours, when time crashes down,
I wonder, do you sit below the cauldron
of night, watching moonlight spill
onto the savage farm and wildflowers appear
as if by incantation, to beguile you
with their slow recital of dreams?

There, as chaotic winds whisper
over the cold lips of the wilderness
faint clues to life's exuberance
and reach, I know you're searching
for lost words of redemption, and hope
you find some with me, where the wild flowers.

THERAPIST

Serial lover, seducer of hearts,
you ply weapons dangerous and keen:
words flashing like stilettos.
You could coax the polestar from the night.
Castanets are playing, as we dance
to rhythms of a sultry flamenco.
I do not always wear the right costume.
As you flay and betray me, I secretly hope
that time wounds all heels. With Freudian sangfroid,
you swear I'm blinded by hindsight.
Crafty, these confidence men.
Whisk! Whisk! Whisk! goes the blade.
You're right, it's a classic case
of mistaken identity. I keep confusing you
with someone who gives a damn.

ALLIES

1

Because we're neighbors on this light-flecked street,
I see a parade of cars in your driveway,
left one by one under the pine, whose cones
litter the ground now like soft hand grenades,
charged with bloom, on a bed of yellow needles.

All day, new members of a shy brigade
I seldom see and never meet, in haste,
climb down to the foxhole of your office
lodged at the azimuth of their unrest—
above the ground, but just below the street.

Sunstruck, their cars blaze like suits of armor.
Or, cloudy days, glow dull as Etruscan mirrors.
Sometimes one waits like a carapace
for the lidless sorrow it conveyed. It's then
my quick heart grows heavy as pewter.

They are fitful or vexed, hostile or wan;
they hear time bombs, they are seeking alms;
they have drunk the long cold gin of self-hate,
found marriage a cang, loved a mirage,
dug toll roads; they are afflicted with themselves.

II

9:00 AM: A woman without her gravity boots
leaves the penitentiary of her car
and, too faint, too light to bear pain's cargo,
floats down the steps, skids wild into your office,
suspended. You anchor her to earth.

3:00 PM: A man tells you his dream
of trees dark as arrowheads, hills spotted
like fawns, geese flying—a flutter of wings.
He takes aim. Fires. The target bursts in midair.
Bloodied, he finds himself in the crosshairs.

5:30 PM: A woman with burnt memories
spills cinders from her mouth, setting the rug
on fire. She finds the past pure mercury—
a puzzle to grasp. With eyes like bright ovens,
she tells you everything she knows.

III

Nomads gripping an abacus of despair,
they engage you to ford plunging rivers
and cross the starless wilderness. Their lives
are dreams whose contents you make visible.
You lead them to the fountains of innocence.

I know these things as I know the dwarf phlox
by your driveway, that started summer
twisted in blood-dark knots, but bloomed last week,
despite the cold calmatives of autumn,
to roaring pink petals and a luminous heart.

I know these things as I know your quaking
aspens and your bittersweet, on icy days
when steam sighs underfoot, lips blue with cold,
and I come to you, shivering, hands cupped
around the brazier of my small, damp soul.

WHERE YOU WILL FIND ME

At sunset, when your large fir
cradles the moon in its arms
and colors surge, remember me,
the caresser of life ever moving,
with a heart full of mischief,
and tense, fragile dreams.

By Atoms
Moved

BY ATOMS MOVED

for Persis Drell

On cool summer mornings, as the pool steams,
Persis and I slip our curves into its
and crawl toward an invisible shore,
churning half an hour into half a mile
of blue, arc over arc. Then we arrive
glad as immigrants at travel's end—a place
we've come to know but can't describe
except with the soft machinery of our limbs.

My mind's abacus always floats away,
so Persis counts the laps, glad to oblige,
since, by day, she hurls the minuscule at speed,
ramming electrons until their guts spill free,
then using numbers to read the entrails,
at the particle accelerator down the road.

When fatigue tugs, we like to rest halfway
and share the odd, busy news of our lives.
It's still a little early for deeper truths.
But swimmable mornings will pivot right
into fall, despite the chill, until leaves fly.
What better place for poet and physicist
to meet than astride waves, dreamily yawning,
somewhere afloat between earth and sky,
on the bright geometry of a summer morning.

THE SUMMER SWIMS

At either shore, the edge seems clear:
a slick blue slide into a paler blue,
the gleaming ladder at the other end.
But, midway along, the world blurs
and time lies still as a paperweight.

Persis and I often swim stroke for stroke,
guiding the soft career of the water
through the hungry turbine of our arms,
but usually she's a few laps ahead;
a shade younger, youth quickens her.

Anyway, there's newborn Joe to be fed
and four-year-old, bug-cuddling Cornelia.
I haven't the same sweet urgencies.
My house will wait however long I dawdle
in motion between the pool's pacific rims.

Because Persis counts laps for both of us,
I finish at full speed and without warning,
through a dreamlike fog that, only in hindsight,
was the last lap tumbling down my face,
as I unmask to drink the opal light.

AUTUMN LAPS

One spanking cold morning, I hear Persis
lightly rattling the garden chain.

She tries to open the gate without noise,
but I know the native racket of the yard:

the wind combed by tree limbs,
the insects at scat-song,

the fierce quarrels and catechisms of birds.
Not even the red-headed woodpecker,

enchanted by the chimney's gonging,
sounds quite the same as Persis

unhitching metal at daybreak.
A buoyant soul, she's come to swim laps

despite the drizzle and falling leaves,
so, slipping into the morning's blue amber,

we dilute our ties to the outside world.
Amphibian in goggles, she varies her stroke,

while I glide face down in mask and snorkel—
a crawling monomaniac. Yet somehow our rhythms overlap.

By now we've pushed miles of water behind us,
paddled hard while the mice of sunrise

poked around the slender trunks of hickories,
and drifted from sleep into a bluer river,

clocking dream laps underground,
before hauling ourselves out dripping and cold

onto that mirrored ledge
where time, work, and love begin again.

BLUESTOCKINGS

Oh lovely girl, once a mischief hound with me
when we twentied through school
as boy-brained, romping word-flingers
who gabbed the telephone wires thin,
studied, craved, shared revelations,
and wrote colorful wind-sprints for poems.

What a pang to see you, decades later,
over nouvelle pizza and cappuccino,
—a beautifully suited, associate dean
at a large rambunctious university,
where you hold the entrails of academics
in perfectly manicured hands.

Married long, mother of two teenage girls
(How did you raise daughters?
We could barely raise ourselves),
you're a distinguished folklorist with a penchant
for fascinating, perfectly researched "smut"
(so the mischief remains!).

As we talk like old friends no longer intimate,
laughing, nostalgic, visibly older,
and our eyes ransack the other's face,
reading lines etched by unshared dramas,
I keep slipping off the rind of the present,
through mind mirage, deep into the theaters of memory.

I see you perfectly then: a young woman
in her padded cell on the ledge of the galaxy,
wide-eyed, foul-mouthed, vision's pupil,
shooting the rapids on an optic nerve;
my wicker self, but in a pink corduroy smock,
analytical and macabre, not yet disabused;

growing bone-tough, and agile as a lizard's tongue,
immune to fear's teeth in desire's throat
draining new loves starch white as old wounds;
eager to pin back the ribs of the world;
seductive as a cipher, and nobody's victim.

But the passing years, the disobedience of distance!
I cheer your victories, wish on your wishes.
Heart's tinder crackles in my words.
You manage to keep a little something in reserve.
We are the same and not the same,
uniquely other, but with pages of shared history.
Like grown sisters, we were young together.

Now accomplished and admirable,
we greet in public clothes, accept invented selves,
mix goodwill with the genteel respect
we save for distinguished strangers,
as we talk ideas, mothers, jobs, old cronies,
avoid the minefield of marriage,
romp a bit, indulge in the cozy pastime
of whatever happened to that scallywag so-and-so.

When you've gone, I dream of flame pots
set out on a moonless runway in darkest Arabia,
and a pilot me piecing together a way home
between the treachery of fog and mountains,
searching down through darkness
for streaks of familiar, precious landmarks
leading to where we might have been.

A HERBAL

for Herbert Leibowitz

When, lucky Herb-ivores, we graze
on bended knees, in praise,
among the fields of Poesy
(where Parnassians like to mosey),
he is always there before us,
erudition massive as a brontosaurus,
his shelf of works growing ever thicker
as tongues wag, pundits bicker,
and critics mill like macrophages.
The poet who, within these pages,
does not appear does not exist.
He shines on them like amethyst.
Look, stranger, on this Herbert now,
adroit at sixty, peerless at the prow.

TRANSITION

In white gowns of winter,
nurses run like chill
down corridors pale as waning
light, to circulate
among the semiprivate rooms
with a quiver of needles:
the calm apaches who broadcast hope.

He watches from the unbearable
comfort of his bed
the lake angering like a shield
in the hazy fall sun.
And he remembers the deer
who leapt into his yard
like lengths of cedarwood
to paw fermented apples
and browse the raspberry shoots.

A piece of him pulls free
and circles with fringed wings
over an Amazon of wires and tinctures
where he lies, to the white smocks
appearing like lilies each day,
to that field of morning glory
where, unbridled, his cells
will soon gallop in all directions.

COMPLAINT ON HER CAT

(A Middle-English Ballad)

Upon my trouthe, I saye you faithfully
My stryped catte, upon the viritoot,
Dragged a toren lesarde in to me
Ageyne, so I hit jugen moot:
A rede-blake heeng and scaled-hoot
Hit was, with smal legges biten deepe.
I heeled hit uppe to weche hit sleepe.

When I putte hit doun al slowly
I was full glad hit was na rat he smoot
Nor byrd agenye, mangled moost cruelly,
Nor snake astrangled lik a roote.
Owne I a catte or lothly stote?
A dai wille comen, and sone, his lepe
Felleth his maistresse, his yren tooth rippe.

A catte scholde pillage and rape stelthily
And ne nevere nat wan in publique smote,
Scholde al pacient be, meeke, and sely,
Nat caterwawe lik a mere-strok stode!
God woot, and I dar wel laye a grote,
Only morne milk and myne gretnesse stoppe
The hard herte that hauteth that softe schape.

viritoot = prowl	stode = stud
jugen = judge	woot = knows
scaled-hoot = scalded hot	grote = bet
sely = holy	hauteth = haunts

Envoy

O grete knitter of al wordes unstronge,
Who chirneth babel into songe,
These uncuth fites unto you I sende
That ye myne whelpe moot wel befrende
When that he straieth from his moder tonge.

FLYING OVER MARTIN'S FERRY, OHIO

for James Wright

I cannot see the men
who work for Wheeling Steel,
but I've studied their towers
and tracks along the river,
steered by their antennae,
breathed the rich smoke
from their factories,
flown through haze
lying like a white drug
across the mountains,
followed their river
as it staggers between states,
a river that catches fire
every autumn, as the men do
in Martin's Ferry, Ohio.

In the light plane I circle
above your hometown, I carry
The Branch Will Not Break
on the seat beside me,
locating the football stadium,
the cemetery, the boxcars, the mills,
and your lines, which quietly
parachute through my cells.

SANTA ANNA'S SURRENDER

According to legend, after the fall of the Alamo to the Mexican dictator Santa Anna, a beautiful mulatta spy named Emily Morgan detained him long enough for Sam Houston to catch him unaware and defeat him easily at San Jacinto.

Take cover here beside me,
   my prince, my Napoleon.
That was nothing but a bird
   signaling day.
My troops are restless!
   Hear them marching in my chest.
Your face looks tense
   as an army on parade.

Come back to bed,
   this slender barracks,
where night grows longer
   the longer you lie
and days are only brief
   prostitutions of clay.

Nothing! The wind!
   A bird tapping in the mesquite.
Nothing! A stray cat
   creeping by the tent poles.

Listen only to the sweet
   artillery of the flesh,
patrol the wilderness of my eyes,

forage in my charms,
spill my hair across your face
like the long hereafter.
Be still, great warrior,
lay down your arms.

WILLIAMSBURG, VIRGINIA

Sad work here:
one-night stanzas
among the magnolia
and the wild holly,
whose dry leaves roll
to three-cornered hats.

Time is stockaded
in the colonial square,
face and hands
locked tight;
nothing will jar them.

I've twisted
the last stars loose
from the sky.

Most nights
the moon is an angry cop,
and I am so lonely
I let him beat me
senseless,
just for the company.

BUYING THE COLLECTED POEMS
OF C. S. LEWIS

Lost friend, I never knew you
when you crouched like a cricket
in fields of tawny sedge,
hymns tumbling from your mouth,
your lips pursed in a silent *Wow*.

You are as dead to me as grain.
I chaff your book in my palms,
its leaves fragile: pinned butterflies:
and, in a store, browse your thoughts
for less than a penny—

how you wrestled with physics,
feared the atom bomb, wooed nature,
and never saw a meteorite fall
without the wide canopy of your mind opening.
Like chalk, your poems light all they touch.

At the heart of things, dust moves
I'm told; yet I'll never join you for chat,
or tea to dim the auroras of fatigue.
An unupholstered voice, a life in outline:
death makes quick work of a half-quenched mind.

Natural
Wonders

NATURAL WONDERS

1

The old moon lying in the young moon's arms

lives in the shadow of her crescent light
and yet he rounds her out, shields her from harm
as she ripens in the star-encrusted night.

Almost a Tao sign, they embrace with limbs
luminous and stark, wedded by less
but braced by design. The arch is their symbol:
a strength made from two weaknesses.

2

When lightning strikes a beach, it burns the sand,

turning it to glass, and those who wander
along the shore find shards of frozen fire
like flattened ziggurats—fossil lightning—
which some call fulgurites, and others know
by names more fanciful or dire, and some think
live inside dragon bones, and still others hold
aloft, to shield their eyes from a sun whose flames
are distant and hotter but kill just the same.

3

In extreme cold, snow forms as diamond dust,

a sun rime I've watched in Antarctic skies
where the surgical wind blows sharp as a scalpel,
the frigid air's too tight to cloud, and yet
moisture ices itself up, cascades and flies
in a continuous shower of spine-tingling sparkle.

Even in winter-waxed New York, flying
through blizzard, often the air's fishbowl clear;
then one can survey from the sky's high shelf
—despite ice-claws, whirlwinds, and gusts—
and see how the battered earth holds herself

calm in time and place and diamond dust.

AMBER

Liquid memory, how gold the prison
trapping this fly undecayed in sunlight,
anatomy pure as any time traveler's.
Once it feasted on rump of mastodon,
then sought shade on a nearby ginkgo tree,
caught unaware by a gemlike sap.
Sweet sticky ooze became its tomb.
Hair-perfect, if slightly mummified,
it flies through our thoughts at dreams per second.
What marvels those compound eyes beheld:
a roman circus of carnivores, slow-motion giants.
In its belly, lie the intact remains
of a last meal: cells of dinosaur,
which may one day climb its DNA
into a world where giants are brick and steel,
and women wear flies in amber
around their necks: tombs within tombs:
ooze of ginkgo tree, blood of dinosaur,
sunhaze on the veldt, liquid memory.

THE CONSOLATION OF APRICOTS

Especially in early spring,
when the sun offers a thin treacle of warmth,
I love to sit outdoors
and eat sense-ravishing apricots.

Born on sun-drenched trees in Morocco,
the apricots have flown the Atlantic
like small comets, and I can taste
broiling North Africa in their flesh.

Somewhere between a peach and a prayer,
they taste of well water
and butterscotch and dried apples
and desert simooms and lust.

Sweet with a twang of spice,
a ripe apricot is small enough to devour
as two hemispheres.
Ambiguity is its hallmark.

How to eat an apricot:
first warm its continuous curve
in cupped hands, holding it
as you might a brandy snifter,

then caress the velvety sheen
with one thumb, and run your fingertips
over its nap, which is shorter
than peach fuzz, closer to chamois.

Tawny gold with a blush on its cheeks,
an apricot is the color of shame and dawn.
One should not expect to drink wine
at mid-winter, Boethius warned.

What could be more thrilling
than ripe apricots out of season,
a gush of taboo sweetness
to offset the savage wistfulness of early spring?

Always eat apricots at twilight,
preferably while sitting in a sunset park,
with valley lights starting to flicker on
and the lake spangled like a shield.

Then, while a trail of bright ink tattoos the sky,
notice how the sun washes the earth
like a woman pouring her gaze
along her lover's naked body,

each cell receiving the tattoo of her glance.
Wait for that moment
of arousal and revelation,
then sink your teeth into the flesh of an apricot.

UNDERWORLD

A red-haired sea creature,
eyes glinting behind the aquarium
of his mask, the guide
tilts a slimy rock on edge
and plucks a starfish
from its den, yanking a leg
so the other four follow.

Twisting his hand sideways
to signal the parrotfish mob,
all eyes at a safe distance,
he lets the star fall
and, for an instant,
thorny legs pedal water.
It drops in slow motion,
belly down, as if ready
to shed its egg swarm into the sea.

Then fish rave in like Serengeti dogs,
tug the chewy spokes off
and drink the innards
while, through the lit séance
of my eyes, horror

tilts another rock
and fills my cupped hands
with brittle stars. Headless,
mindless, all mouth and leg,
they flail when I grab them,

are baffled to be alive.
One I set on a coral polyp,
urging it toward a rock slit below,
a tooth ahead of a pearjack,
three yellowtails,
and hungry, raisin-finned Mr. Bones.
Two, tumbling from my grip,
are swallowed whole by damselfish.

Steady, steady, I tell myself.
It's okay. You would not have these fish
with their gaunt, level eyes
go empty-bellied another day,
nor rid the world of the eel's muddy gloaming
when from its soft length
generations spurt, or miss
the tottering meander of a calf,
or a new dahlia's rooty mayhem.
Marvels spring from hecatombs and waste.

But, hours later, the brittle stars
and death grinding to cold
the cuddle warmth of all matter,
gives me such poor peace
as no flim-flam of renewal,
no sop-tossing of rowdy miracles
will cure, even if things
work just as I suppose,
and the hand on the trigger
rigs the ripening rose.

ECLIPSE

The black dogs of hell
are chasing down the sun
whose horns pour light,
hooves cut sparks,
eyes weep the clement sap
rippling through our veins
that keeps the heart limber
and the seasons sane.

The runner stumbles.

The air stiffens like a tomb.
Butchered light staggers
across the sea. Then day fails,
time eases its grip
and, thrashing, the world reels
upside down
as stars pant on the horizon
like a regiment of wolves.

The runner stumbles.

Darkness falls at noon.
The cold fabrics of night
cascade through skies
fantastic and grim.
A cloud cortege struts
above the ancient ruins,
where planets appear
like silent drumbeats.

The runner stumbles.

A door opens to the ghost towns
of our past, and we pray
that nothing will phase the sun
undulating
through our crops,
tethering our clocks,
sweeping the nightmares
from our dreams.

The runner stumbles.

We would sacrifice anything
—our wealth, our limbs,
our power, our kin—
to ransom that hot-blooded,
infernal mate, so rash
and unruly, immense as life,
crooning fire,
that sweet cheat, that savage light.

The runner resumes.

SOME WOULD MARRY WINTER

Some would marry winter
when the plainsong of the trees
fills the woods
with a stark, simple melody
of land and light,
the vintner fall has faded
to cold sobriety,
and pious winds intone
the grace notes of infinity.

I prefer the summer vows
of bluejay and raccoon,
the fidget of bugs
while May half swoons
flamboyantly into the arms of June,
the pretty pandemonium
of skitter and bloom,
and even warthogs making love
under a fat August moon.

AVIATRIX

In dawn's feathered light,
a lady cardinal hurls herself
against my bedroom window.

Hallucinations stalk the glass
as she slams her softness
into a flat, cold world,

trying to perch on a limb
perfect in the sunlight,
but it will not hold her
skidding feet, her urgent thumping.

The hours are long panes
of glass she cannot enter.
Love wings through
another world without her.

Tomorrow, it will begin again,
only louder, the frantic pounding
of her feathery will,

the grinding down of her notes,
one by one, in the glare of reflection,
where loneliness stuns her.

UNREQUITED POEM

Fuse the invisible angles
of life's rialto,
build a jetty from the boardwalk
into the ambiguous Atlantic,
make a landmark of love
in a fen of misgiving,
steer a caravan of small daily marvels
through the architecture of annihilation,
and you will have a poem:
an outpost in the vast margins of snow
where nomads meet for a moment
to feast, despite the stale gaze of the tundra.

In this unrequited poem, a gazebo stands in a Japanese garden in St. Louis. From its bench, you can see a shagbark hickory, blunted off at twelve limbs, holding forth a spray of new branches. It's inevitable; the spring.

There you imagine the quiet shocks of vision you know to be possible. For example, the lacy black twigs of the hickory, each noded and razory clear against the sky. For ten years, you've been trying to capture their rigid frilliness. Something about that delicate collar lace imposed on a sky blue as mosque tile fills you with tenderness. Something suggested by the stark precision of the twigs, which you can't seem to pinpoint.

But when you do, the front door of the gazebo will close, the latch marry the lock and, inside, a dozen circling dogs will lie down for a slender moment, serene at last beneath the blue aerodrome of the sky.

So you go on trying to build the poem, maybe in prose
whose rafters are longer, or perhaps in the clipped gestures
you began with:

A gazebo in a Japanese garden
in St. Louis. From its bench,
you see a shagbark hickory,
blunted off at twelve limbs, holding forth
a spray of new branches. . . .

YOU WILL THINK THIS A DREAM

Headline over an article about the invention of
electricity, Ladies' Home Journal, *1915*

Hypnotized, it leaps
through coiled metal
to drive cauldrons wild
in a parenthesis of flame.

Stroke the wall
and daylight breaks.
Twist a dial,
summer purrs through.
With pocket inferno,
light a cigarette
from the succinct chaos
with which the Universe began.

But in night's other country,
where time is mirage,
fire was an animal
whose gold flanks scorched
and whose galloping
devoured grasslands as it fled.
No one tamed lions,
no one dreamed of narrowing
frenzy in its flight.

How shall I explain
to my ancient self
the invisible fires

we train now as pets,
let alone the genie locked
in all living things?

How explain the hibiscus,
geranium and lily
thriving in tropical deceit
at my window, beyond which
the park lies drab and frozen?

In a landscape invisible
in time and space,
I can aim the enemy,
I can pipette the sun.
To the lily it's Africa—
rampant heat and showers.
But more than glass
protects the hothouse flowers.

Tender
Mercies

TENDER MERCIES

for W. H. Auden

Love, no one's enemy, forgiving all
who dare its rapids with even half an oar,
the angel in the house, the medic at the war—
for penance or pardon, they yearn to fall.
My land, the cunning; my word, the power.
My clock keeps running and spilling the hours
that are nobody's burden, everyone's load.
Somewhere in that sandglass love is stowed,
shifting and settling, in creases, in corners,
in the feet of the bellman, in the grip of the mourners.
It's the best sort of trouble (everyone has a story).
Every heart has a myth that keeps it from glory.
It's a beast and a bother, a landslide of hurts,
yet a feast, and the only halo that fits.

THE THIEF OF ALWAYS

Sweet friend, you send words down my spine
despite the mercury on this gnat-fattening day
when summer sweats in the trees,
hawks carry the sky upon their shoulders,
and the lilacs are hung with chalk shadows.
Never will my green hankering draw you near,
not in summer, whose loon-long serenade
whispers through the lunatic thrill of breezes,
not when spring floods the trees with petaled rain,
not in winter, when the wrens fly against the scolding wind.

Nothing like manna will fall from your eyes
into my gaping heart, whose spinning
drives me to my knees. Clutching the hot poker
of prayer, I crouch beside nettles,
and dare hope the way blind horses leap.
How I long to hold your face like a bouquet
and inhale the mysterious scent of your dreams
when the summer grass is green as a dye.
Encircled by your arms, I would take flight,
my hips flap like herons in slow even beats.

Of course, in time, that boiler-down of savory days,
night will narrow my heart's best schemes
and drain the world-bright fever from my bones.
Then, sure as autumn, my love will rot,
cell by sound, hearth by bone, while trumpets gush
the silent noise of stays, and the thief of always
carries me away from the world's sweet mischief

and stammering pride, from the what-ifs
fluttering like maypole ribbons
around the mast of your incontrovertible love.
In time, night will settle my heart's hash,
slug through regret, set all to rest, and rub even
the steepest cares away. In time. But not today.

SEARCHING FOR THE COMET

In the bright night of stars, they stood
on a wooden deck behind the bungalow,
searching for the comet that would appear
in tailless mastery through the open neck
of the Milky Way, blazing out
only to return to emptiness,
but in between riveting the sky with fire.
His arm arced around her waist,
they stood watching the crystal blackness
and the pinprick light of suns, thinking:
oh, the freedom of the day that yielded
to no rule or time, a day flung
from the orbit of their lives,
in which they drank from the well
of kisses for hours, set brush fires
in each other's limbs, and soared
above the flat world they mapped
with families a continent away,
oh, the cool compress of the evening,
the staggering fires of the day.

NOT THINKING OF YOU

Yes, the hot-blooded sun
yanking crocuses up upon their roots.

But no, your wild unbridled eyes
galloping hell-for-leather into mine.

Yes, the bloom-luscious magnolia tree
drunk with pale, brandy-snifter flowers.

But no, my spine's soft riverbed,
which you again and again and again kissed.

Yes, the fog rolling in off the lake
at nightfall, under the tolling of the stars.

But no, the blur of our knotted fingers.
No, the well water of your deep-rolling kisses.

No, the love-brightened room you fled
for the tight, local orders of your life.

No, my whisperless bed when you'd gone,
where I lay till dawn opened

red arms on the horizon and, in my chest,
nothing like day began breaking.

SAN FRANCISCO SUNRISE

My mother once watched
the junks in Kowloon Bay
stretch pale wings
like awakening egrets,
as they shook themselves
free of night chill.
I come from a long line
of mystics and marvelers.

Now, opening the sheer drapery
eyelids of dawn,
I see a harbor sparkling,
barges lit like constellations,
as I slip into the mauve blouse
of the morning, a cascade of light
too voluminous to bear.

The day breathes heavily,
its lungs thick with fog.
Ships are ingots
on a pastel smear of bay.
Because the sky has no horizon,
water pours into its own arms.
Night-roaming eyes
begin to cluster on the bridges.

When sun-spit hits
the skyscraper windows,
dark rainbows creep

like scarab beetles,
then the powerhouse sun,
risen at last, jolts the city
brilliants to life.

It's calmer to look away,
not swallow the light whole,
but I crave its riveting heat
and molten tears, its lifebloom
and bomb-bright hurrahs.
For last night I dreamed death
pawing at my chest—an invisible beast
with an antler of stars.

SEASONING

Because the gods are baking winter cakes
powdered sugar sifts over the yard
in slow motion, hushed as thought.
Bare trees resemble sticks of cinnamon.
And I remember the gingerbread house
my mother and I built in Illinois
one snowy afternoon when I was six.

Oh, the smell of the fresh-baked walls!
We frosted its pungent roof with white
until vanilla icicles dribbled
from the eaves onto gumdrop bushes
and bottlebrush trees. Then I pressed a toy
calf and sheep into the snow, waiting
as it hardened and they were firmly held
by pure sweetness, like this memory.

THE LONGING

Waking at night,
still singing the sleep song of the mind,
I jot down this dream
(everything but the longing):

Strolling hand in hand
through a forest of pine and hickory,
while ferns caress our knees,
we feel anything but longing.

Our hearts grow wild as tinder,
passionate and tender,
as we sample love's banquet,
feasting on longing.

Overhead, butterflies sail
in a panorama of wings,
like small fluttering calendars
whose days dispel longing.

The night fills with panting ravens
and somnambulisms of light.
Nuzzled between my breasts
you hear hoofbeats, not longing.

Under a blanket of stars,
we wrap our hearts around each other
and let the dawn enthrall us
with silenced longing.

Suddenly I wake from paradise
to the cold clay of truth,
land of heartache and strife,
and plummet deep into longing.

Touching my lips,
which your dream lips last kissed,
I find them wet as blood oranges
and delirious with longing.

But for the longing
my heart would drink
several dazzles a day,
and spend the loose change
of the evening on prayer.

But for the longing
I would gallop across dust and blood.
Now what shall I do
with my standstill heart?

If you cannot love me, teach me.
In my dialect they are the same,
differing only in inflection.
Both are graced by longing.

Many will come to love you.
I will come to leave you,
the sorrow dance we danced,
and all the bright catastrophes—
everything but the longing.

RETURN TO CHARLOTTESVILLE

Like summer light
you shine everywhere
along the roads and in the fields,
in the huge sky's thunder pockets
full of bright change.

The last time I came here
you were alive, a young pilot
earning hours
like long loaves of bread.
Then you crashed. Torn up,
I wrote your epitaph.

The geese honking
on the lake
know a hundred songs
of wind and sky,
but sing none of them to me.

At dawn tomorrow
I'll go ballooning:
a slow, dazzling ascent
in the liquid cool of the day,
while I try to pull
the sky through my arms,
try to rise above
the weight of your memory.

AFTERTHOUGHT

Toadies thick as an Egyptian plague
line your office each afternoon.
Wit-lame and mincing, they backpat or effuse.
People stop in the hallways to discuss your mood—
the deft, the spoonfed, those with brains of rattan.
Stricken, I wince as you rally each
with well-tried, if tonic, deceits.
Sweet years, I rode your faith's catamaran,
thought I'd a special affection specially won.
When my metal fretted, lest it fly apart,
I coiled you round the mainspring of my heart.
But you were lukewarm to me as to any other,
nesting your indifference in charm.
All the while I flourished in your countenance,
you gulled me, you led me a dance,
wooed me as protégée, lady-love, confrère,
when you never cared, you never cared.

LASCAUX

Under gem-black logs
sleeved in flame,
embers glow like live tissue.
As I hunch closer
to warm my palms by hearth light,
sparks become bees
painted in ocher
on a Cro-Magnon's wall.

Suddenly old and frantic as the sun,
I want to dip my fingers
into cool thick clay
and draw quagga, bison, deer
on the ceiling, shaggy ungulates,
a hickory in fruit . . .

. . . which is how
you come to find me here,
naked before the fire,
the Icelandic sheepskin
yanked off the wall,
its aromatic fur
clutched to my breasts,
as I watch flames
willow up into blackness
and my pupils grow wild as kindling.

ON LOCATION IN THE LOIRE VALLEY
(a ghazal)

Clouds of mistletoe hang in the poplars, which can't survive.
Still, decorated with ruin, they enchant our lives.

In stone castles, cold's steel roars straight up the spine,
and, shivering to the core, we decant our lives.

For one minute of dead quiet, the restlessness stops.
"Room tone." Soundmen record the silent rant of our lives.

Together we consort with chance, cascade through time.
Each trip we find ourselves on the gallivant of our lives.

After a whole life in miniature: naive start, work, friends,
even a small death at the end, we adjourn to the constant of
    our lives.

How we stumble at good-byes, as if we felt nothing for no one,
heartless to the bone. Quiet meals, quick farewells dismantle
    our lives.

At home, we regale loved ones with adventures half-true.
Night drives through fog nonchalant as our lives.

Alone with legendary art, herding sheep at St. Michel,
the wizardries of smell . . . all was banter in our lives.

The heart has a curfew. We can tell folk where and how we
    were,
but we cannot tell them who. What a pantomime, our lives.

Not the shadow family we became, not the shiver beneath the
    smile,
not the people we clung to in the mad canter of our lives.

City of
Dreams

CITY OF DREAMS

City of paper floating between seas,
where slow-motion giants pump iron underground
  and fog pours from a panting mouth
below the street; petrified city, city of amber sap
  sealing a million lives in one drop;

city of grime, where the weekends
wash ashore each Monday morning;
  whose pilgrims, arriving by steamer,
lived like cattle and kings, and still do—
  the poor in steerage, the rich high above;

city of flesh, whose ribs arch above rivers,
whose organs gleam, where animal life spills
  from the streets and the gutters are blood canals;
city where the lightest decision or indecision
  feeds a dozen men with martinis and knives;

city of art, where one's fingers grow extra joints,
learn to bend sideways and break without pain;
  where people gallop like horses to the fence
of a relationship, the sanctuary of a thigh, the waterhole
  where the birdlike mate in mirrors;

city of signs, whose people dream
the American Dream (to belong everywhere to everyone),
  but settle for a neighborhood;
city where spores blowing in from the country
  fill dry sinuses with hope, and a blade of grass

bursting through mortar or brick
  becomes concrete as winter, city of grit;

  city of wire, where even the indolent and icy
can live hot on the senses, grasping the inner electric
  of city life like a third rail, then breathing fire
until their lips spark; city whose lights blossom at nightfall,
  city of neon gardens and time verandas;
city of tides, city of glass, tribal city, city of masks;
  fiesta city, over which an invisible piñata spins.

PUMPING IRON

Across the gym
a man sweats,
cheeks puffing
to work the bellows
of his will,
his eyes silent carcasses
as he heaves
raw metal
to the moment of will-shed,
groans, and swallows
his toad of disgust.

She sighs.
A trainer drills
her hot, slurring arms.
She strains.
A hollow sough fills the air.
"What were you
in your first incarnation?"
she gasps.
His eyes pin her
to the steel throne
of the machine.
"The same," he whispers.

Elbows wide, she flaps
till muscles
quiver and fail.
Then thought drops

its cang from her neck
and pain is the gossip
of some other body.

Outside, a cartouche
of rabbit tracks
in the snow
becomes too faint
an image to recall.

GRAMERCY PARK

The odd career
of the wind
has baffled the sycamore
to autistic rocking,

as a garage attendant
tosses salt
from a red can.
He might be sowing.

Indoors,
jungle flowers
ache into bloom
on the windowsill,
an equator of color
all trade route
and Amazon,

where a woman sits
between two schemes,
watching a blue city
grow even more metallic,
and the mute clouds
pull themselves apart.

HUNGARIAN WOMAN ON ELLIS ISLAND, 1907

Photographed by Louis Hine

Rumpled from steerage,
she wears an embroidered blouse
and seventeen petticoats
whose hems hide money,
documents, even love letters.

Renewal is the private fortune
she brings, learned partly
in steerage's carnival of filth
where five hundred sailed for weeks
in one shuddering, bolting room,
seasick all the way
on soup and stale biscuits;
gagging on bad air, tobacco,
fruit rinds, garlic, and sweat;
sleeping on cork life preservers,
but mainly awake for rats
and the rhythmic clatter
of metal railings and hawsers.

She half expected to find
a golden turnstile ahead,
or two gigantic gates spread open
in embrace, not an island fortress
floating in mist off Manhattan
whose skyline she first mistook
for a mountain range.

Clean-shaven American men
herded her through mazes and exams,
at one low lifting her eyelids
with buttonhooks, at another
feeding her ladlefuls of prunes.
When they cropped her name
it was a kind of circumcision.

What else had she left
but her only heirloom, *Grenstovak?*
Green fell from the clouds
and she slipped it on,
because America was her open sesame
to a world honeyed with drama,
full of dreamers and risk takers,
and Ellis Island the eye of a needle
through which she wished
to pass the camel of her hope.

In this photograph
posed with stoic candor
outside the Main Hall
where all wait for the ferry ride
through slick waters,
she holds her bundles and child
as if balancing separate thoughts.
Dark as horse chestnuts,
her eyes seem to shout.

She does not know that she will give birth
to poets and farmers,
astronauts, sales corps, tamers of cities.

All that is distant haze in 1907.
When the photographer finishes,
she looks at the mint-green saint in the harbor,
and vows that its long gesture
from earth to sky
will be the path she blazes,
her torch to time.

Cantos
Vaqueros

CANTOS VAQUEROS

I

Merejildos Gutierrez,
(how can I call you
a name you rarely use,
a name like an heirloom vest
hot weather and work
make stifling to wear?).

In your swerve of desert,
where nothing I've banked on
or badgered applies, I can't read
the sun-drugged anatomy
of the land, or ride like a parson,
press a herd, rope at speed,
drive a truck through mud wallows,
engineer a windmill, mend a prolapsed cow.

And though, like the flair
for these arts, it roams
through you indivisibly as breath,
your humor's a tough dialect
for me to master, a tempo-drunk song
with a jazz of laughter
I can't quite catch
the rhythm and swing to.

Part Portuguese, part Indian,
your name shortens
to *Mere,* a workaday word

stubborn as a boot heel kicking dirt.
Saying it, you smoothly tilt the "r"
then slide down to a voiced hollow.

Club-tongued, I scrape along
by calling you *Mettie,*
but I suppose it's fitting
I can't pronounce your name
since, after all, I can't pronounce your life.

II

On a palomino with moods
sharp as quills,
you'll be herding now:
spurs, felt hat,
weathered chaps with silver conchas
accenting each leg
and one ripped pocket
revealing a heart of red suede,
your arms so mapped
with freehand tattoos
it's hard to tell
blue ink from blue vein.

How I long to devour
a heavy ranch breakfast again
(not yours: three eggs,
bacon, toast, milk,
no coffee, three more eggs),
then tug on my chaps,

trailer the horses,
climb into that pickup truck
you spit and polish like agate,
and rumble off, radio blaring,
to patrol the pastures—
living on horseback
where one can see so far
yet so little—mesquite, cactus, yucca, and sage;
where land can be quirky
and miles disappear
as a distant rider or truck gathers
the fabric of the plains.

From afar, the vista heals over
and becomes the same—
mesquite, cactus, yucca, and sage—
and objects vanish. Where are the truck,
the rider, the waterhole?
Once like coarse black pepper
they speckled the horizon;
now, spinning, you are lost.

III

My heart pleads for the blue-white fever
of high noon, caramel mesas,
stinkweed, and mother-snuggling calves,
the creaky drawl of windmills
snoring in the distance,
Adelina's hell-seeded chili peppers,
all the postures of rest

(leg curled around a saddle horn,
lying under a pickup truck,
one boot heel angled off a low fence board,
in the shade cast by a horse,
squatting anywhere . . .),
for beans, tortillas,
slabs of fresh beef, saffron cake,
iced tea and hard work,
the dungeony smell of sagebrush,
fragrant as a pomander
when you chaff it in your hand,
the loon's cry of a cowboy
down in the creekbed
wrangling the day's horses,
and the butter-churned bloom
of prairie sunflowers
forged out of heat on the anvil land.

IV

Sundogs circle my eyes:
soon a brewing storm
will uproot the watergaps I set,
wire by wire, in calmer weather.
Mere, I wish I could ride
with you now on the brawly palominos
you prefer hot-blooded as the land
but train to lope slowly
as a gold ripple on water,
tempers hushed, lulling your bones
through long days in the saddle

on a wind-whisked prairie
where tree cacti clump ornery green fists
and tiny flowers
rig parched roots in blind need.

V

A land terse as an epigram,
the desert wakes
to pounding incantations of light.
By noon I wipe the sweat
from my eyes, my papery mouth pouts
to whistle the herd,
and the air staggers with a heat
no night on earth could sober up again.

Though tonight, clear as a bobcat's eye,
will lay a cold compress
along the sunstruck plains,
tomorrow the solar opus will resume,
shadows grow short
and inky as eighth notes,
arpeggios of color scale the mesa walls.

Watching from these margins
of thought, I imagine you loping
between the waterholes,
in a liquid heat that blurs work and sleep
and leaves no shade anywhere.
No hay sombra donde quiera. Como vida,
you once lamented. No relief

from the acid rivers of the sun.
No relief from the fiery spasms of the heart.

VI

When at last I bleach into the dust
I sprang from I pray I will wake
to no fat oasis no palace of plenty
no tranquil white fog no numb peace.
When I shed this life where wonder
was my job as yours was cowboying
I pray I will wake on a bustling ranch
where trailers shimmy in high wind
the sun pours like lye and the sight of the mesas
at sunrise with Venus howling loud
flings my soul into parabolas of delight
as I saddle up to work bone-weary on horseback
earning my rest my water my dalliance
while rising and setting with the sun.

VII

Clad in this New York November
where, foil-bright,
the yard smacks of Christmas
(disheveled red ribbons, gold lamé wrap),
where Chaplinesque squirrels
mime in the grass,
mountain ranges, moneyed with gold
and copper, here and there divulge
a lone pink tree

standing flamingo-like in the woods,
and abrupt winds
all crescendo and swoon
pitch you
from one elation to the next,
I can't find my jubilee spirits anywhere.
Despite the glacial lake
and the color-mad season, I hear little
from that gabby inmate of my ribs.

Mere, when next you ride
your feisty palomino,
herding from sunflower lowlands
up to mesa meadows of tall grass,
funneling swarmy cows
through narrow gates
and whisking strays along
like bits of breadcrumb,
keep watch for a scintillation
in the dust, a twist of metal
no bigger than a mainspring.

You may see it splashing the air
with umber wings,
feel it in the reedy buzz
of the crickets, hear it
as a cowboy bays to the herd.
It may spook your horse
into a waltz gait to tease you.
It may call you *vaquero*
and sip ice water

from your pickup's canteen.
It may whisper from my namesake,
the moon, when like a solitary walker,
she raises her face to heaven.
It may douse its sweat-ribboned breasts
with water, and swim
like a gypsy of the wells.

Next time you ride out
to toss salt, fix windmills,
restring barbed wire
saggy after a flood,
patrol the fattening herd
and the waterholes,
or hunt arrowheads
and the old bottles you collect,
keep watch for starry metal
lying in the brush
—a mood of me
that felt at home
where genius is physical,
one needn't shy
from being brave, and where,
out of my element,
I felt husked of all expectations.

To a manicured mind
that fidgets with ideas
like a terrier ragging a favorite shoe,
what could be more thrilling
than sense-drenched days
smoothed by hard work?

VIII

One morning, as I closed the cyclone-fence gate
to begin a slow drift
down to the cookhouse on foot
(because my truck wheels were glued
in deep mud once again),
I walked straight into
the waiting non-arms of a snake,
its tan beaded-bag skin
studded with black diamonds.

Up it coiled to speak at eye level.
Imagine! that sleek finger
rising out of the land's palm
and coiling faster than a Hindu rope.
The thrill of a bull snake
startled in the morning
when the mesas lie pooled
in a custard of light
kept me brighter than ball lightning all day.

Praise leapt first to mind
before flight or danger,
praise that knows no half-truth, and pardons all.

IX

If heart permits,
do not remember harshly
this pale alien
who swept into your ranch like a fever,

this question-mad woman
who knew so little
of custom and etiquette,
made a clumsy *vaquera,*
bedeviled you, perplexed you,
rolled the fiber of your life
between her fingers,
lit it up and smoked.

And if sometimes I seemed
more willing than wise,
I am not a reckless woman.
Most often I tremble quietly
while the dazzling caravan
parades its horns and drums
and cartwheels of light,
its lemurs, and bulls, and tropical birds
so blue they make your ribs quiver,
all its fizzy young hooligan horses,
its calypsos and dirges,
boogie-woogies and psalms,
clown-paint, fidget, confetti and rapture.
I hug the curb,
crowd-safe, as I should.
But now and then,
I must leap astride a palomino,
grab the mane
when bullied by qualms, but march
amid the ballyhoo and the glitter.

For if I won't leap up
and ride, who will?

And, if no one will ride,
when at last the spangly caravan is over,
silence rules,
and we are left staring
across an empty street
into the blank of each other's eyes,
who will tell about the drums
and the cartwheels of light?
Who will say
what marvel it was swept by?

X

I don't see your silhouette
anywhere—standing swaybacked
a touch bowlegged,
with frijole-brown chaps
and spurs two North Stars.
A hundred times I've seen you
spit a comet of tobacco juice,
tilt your hat, then plant gloved hands
on your hips, knuckles folded under.
A hundred times I've watched you
riding down an arroyo
or loping up a creekbed wall,
your horse's rump tolling like a bell.

Must be I find you
tough and lusty as the life,
all toil and tempo,
finesse and plain fight,
with values so old they startle me.

Must be I think of you
as I do the rugged flowers
that prove themselves over and over in the spring,
that elsewhere might perish,
but here master the earth,
bloom into gangly lives of high color,
and inhale the sun, knowing the land
better than the land does.
Hardy, savvy,
they will outlive us all.

BOOKS BY DIANE ACKERMAN

DEEP PLAY

Ackerman introduces the state of transcendence she calls deep play, a state of unselfconscious engagement with our surroundings that draws from us our finest performances and taps into the faculties that make us feel most fully alive. She shows us that understanding deep play, and some of the ways it is attained, is understanding how lives filled with joy, creativity, and self-fulfillment are sustained.

Nonfiction/0-679-77135-2

I PRAISE MY DESTROYER
Poems

Divided into seven sections, including "Timed Talk," "By Atoms Moved," and "Tender Mercies," *I Praise My Destroyer* is less an assorted poetry collection than an organically coherent whole, one that reveals Ackerman's true calling as a twentieth-century metaphysical poet of the highest order.

Poetry/0-679-77134-4

JAGUAR OF SWEET LAUGHTER
New and Selected Poems

Ackerman's Olympian vision records and transforms landscapes from Amazonia to Antarctica, while her imaginative empathy penetrates the otherness of hummingbirds, deer, and trilobites. Her poems are indelible reminders of what it is to be a human being—the "jaguar of sweet laughter" that, according to Mayan mythology, astonished the world because it was the first animal to speak.

Poetry/0-679-74304-9

THE MOON BY WHALE LIGHT

Whether she's sexing an alligator barehanded or coaxing a bat to tangle in her hair, Diane Ackerman goes to unique—and sometimes terrifying—extremes to observe nature at first hand. Provocative, celebratory, and wise, *The Moon by Whale Light* is a book that forges extraordinarily visceral connections between the reader and the natural world.

Nature/0-679-74226-3

A NATURAL HISTORY OF LOVE

From aphrodisiacs in ancient Egypt to Sigmund Freud, from Abelard and Heloise to *Blade Runner*, the poet and naturalist delivers an exuberant, scientific, anecdotal tour of the "great intangible"—love in its many forms.

Nonfiction/0-679-76183-7

A NATURAL HISTORY OF THE SENSES

In the course of this grand tour of the realm of the senses, Ackerman tells us about the evolution of the kiss, the sadistic cuisine of eighteenth-century England, the chemistry of pain, and the melodies of the planet Earth with an evocativeness and charm that make the book itself a marvel of literate sensuality.

Nonfiction/0-679-73566-6

THE RAREST OF THE RARE
Vanishing Animals, Timeless Worlds

With the insatiable curiosity and lavish powers of description that have made her our foremost naturalist-poet, the author journeys in search of monarch butterflies and short-tailed albatrosses, monk seals and golden lion tamarin monkeys: the world's rarest creatures and their vanishing habitats. She delivers a rapturous celebration of other species that is also a warning to our own.

Nature/0-679-77623-0

A SLENDER THREAD

In this intimate and compassionate record of her service as a counselor on a suicide and crisis hotline, Ackerman turns her attention to the troubled lives of those suffering from what she calls the "small demonology of our age"—anxiety, depression, and all the trials, uncertainties, and conflicts of love.

Nonfiction/0-679-77133-6

VINTAGE BOOKS
Available at your local bookstore, or call toll-free to order:
1-800-793-2665 (credit cards only)